DARKNESS NEVER FAR

MATTHEW FREEMAN

coffeetownpress

Seattle, WA

Published by Coffeetown Press
PO Box 95462
Seattle, WA 98145

All rights reserved. No part of this book may be reproduced or transmitted in any form or by any means, electronic or mechanical, including photocopying, recording, or any information storage and retrieval system, without permission in writing from the publisher.

Cover design by Sabrina Sun

Cover art by Antonia Webb

Contact: info@Coffeetownpress.com

Copyright © 2010 by Matthew Freeman.

ISBN: 978-60381-063-0 (Paper)
ISBN: 978-1-60381-101-9 (Cloth)

The specific quality of human sexuality has nothing to do with the immediate, rather stupid, reality of copulation, including the preparatory mating rituals; it is only when animal coupling gets caught in the self-referential vicious circle of the drive, in the protracted repetition of failure to reach the impossible Thing, that we have what we call sexuality, that sexuality itself becomes sexualized.

Slavoj Zizek

The text, in short, is a fetish ... and to reduce it to a unity of meaning by a deceptively univocal reading is to cut the braid, to sketch the castrating gesture.

Roland Barthes

I would mention that, as always, I was entangled in urgent cases as I wrote this.

Jacques Lacan

Contents

Preface i

PRESENT   1

    I Guess You Call it Clarity 1
    Heavy Metal Mike 3
    Pass 12
    Reading Sonnet 13
    Ass-Kicking, Delivered at Blueberry Hill 14
    Promo 16
    Vampires 17
    What People Think 18
    Brevity on Broadway 19
    Oceans Can Belong 20
    No Sleep Until Sauget (for Amanda G.) 21

ABSENT   23

    Barroom Veteran 25
    Piss Poor Parenting 26
    The Return to Repression 28
    Anhedonia as the Letter W 30
    To the Other Side 32
    Morons, Getting Wasted 33
    Finally Get Born 34
    Six Months on the Chain Gang 35
    Cascado for Hope and Amanda 36

The Most Hated Poet in St. Louis 38
I Was All that Was Left of the World 40
Thoughts 41
Opposing Transference 42
Progress 43
"Gay for Pay" 44
Maudit 45
Hobo Repression Blues 48
After the Praecox 49
Senses 50
Some Words 51

FINISHED 53

3rd Song, New Dorm 55
Amanda Laughing 56
It Makes Me Wanna Puke 57
Hard Times Lounge 59
Hard Times and Bathsheba 60
Discourse of the Delmar Hysteric 62
"Oh Narrow is the Way" 63
Mooching for Two 65
You Might be a Schizophrenic 66
Dear Phone Company, ... 69
I'm Normal, God Said 71
Magdalene 72
A Heartbeat from Homeless 74
She Doesn't Like Me and There's a Tear in My Soda 75

Preface

Darkness Never Far is an exploration into the thoughts and feelings of an individual who has visited the darkest places of the human heart. Fortunately, the author has now returned to teach the rest of us important lessons about human love and longing. Matthew Freeman was my patient many years ago—and I wondered then whether he would find the peace and happiness every person deserves. After reading *Darkness Never Far*, it is apparent that he is still seeking that peace. Matthew's latest book of poems takes us on a journey through the streets of St. Louis, so that we can look through his eyes at women, men, authority, medicine, hopelessness, and hope. In many poems, Matthew explores relationships between the obvious and the hidden in life. There is pain, cruelty, gentleness, rejection, and finally acceptance in his journey. He generously invites us to accompany him on his journey, but we are challenged to look straight on at the feelings one encounters when one is left out—perhaps put to the side as expendable.

Some of Matthew's poems are edgy, while others are whimsical. For St. Louisans, they hold a special gift—Matthew's descriptions of St. Louis streets and establishments are vivid and recall the smells, sounds, and other sensations of these wonderful places.

I have worked with patients who struggle with mental illnesses my entire adult life, and many reach deep into themselves to share their experiences with all of us through the arts. Certainly, the drive to create in this way can be part of a useful healing process. However, it is more than coincidence that creativity often goes hand-in-hand with extremes of mood and departures from reality. Some now say that mental illness is the price the human species must pay for creativity. What is meant here is that the "abnormal" ways of thinking and behaving that we recognize as symptoms of a mental illness exist on a continuum of behavior that runs across the entire human population. In the middle of this continuum, we find creativity and original thinking—a benefit to us all. But if one explores the extremes of the continuum, there we find individuals who struggle to reconcile their experiences and beliefs with accepted realities. The thoughts of such individuals may be out of step with the experiences of others, but they are nonetheless full of meaning for the rest of us.

Matthew Freeman has given us a gift of insight in *Darkness Never Far*. It will help those to continue to struggle with mental illness, those who are the family members and loved ones of psychiatric patients, and those who have dedicated themselves to improving the lives of patients and their families.

John G. Csernansky, M.D.
Gilman Professor and Chair, Department of Psychiatry and
    Behavioral Sciences
Northwestern University Feinberg School of Medicine

PRESENT

I Guess You Call it Clarity

My double would've left behind a kid,
he would've been some type of clear physicist
with clean fingers in front of a stupored class
and a red or black car with a brunette beautiful
from church authentic and into Washington Irving
and silver bracelets smart and creative—the pain—
he would've been calm and quiet in great tweed and musk
walking the clean university halls and
pretty clear concerning the minds of God
his wife would've
let her hair flow witty and wear
intelligent dresses and Flaubert and Christianity
somehow she had also been a Rams cheerleader
in her twenties what, supportive
with great friends and recipes and
poor verses in love with her, my double
would've perceived things a lot more clearly
and enjoyed life more and been proud
when his son walked and not beat him or break windows
his big red or black car and his wife would've
provoked titanic proportions of envy
but he would've remained figurative and calm
and would've had a couple
of drinks at a faculty party
and stole away with a rival's wife
and had sex with her in his red or black car
and the mirrors would've fogged up
though he could still have sensed the quadrangle and awards
and he would've driven home afterwards
to the great professorial house with lots of dark wood
and lame-ass pseudo-literary books all around
but on the way home the
lights would've been completely clear

as he passed the dorms
full of English majors who wanted him
and he would've never done drugs or
been committed to an asylum or drunk tank
he would've been a completely sure Christian
somehow sensing easily right and wrong
and forgiveness in his head but lots of sex
his shoes would've been nice brogues
but clarity and sensations while on sundays
he ran around the track and had
two beers only and listened to Prairie Home Companion
replayed and maybe a football game
he would never have
driven too fast or talked too much
he would've been calm and detested cigarettes
but would he have died?
Well, I guess everyone dies.
But how did he die and what did he see?
He would've left behind some kids and money
a string of affairs and donations and a plaque or two
and so I wonder about all this clarity
and whether he submitted or I submitted and to what
and just who has what power and what continuity
and if everybody contains his opposite
and also, when you get down to it,
what some half-assed physicist ever accomplished,
I mean, even the greatest mathematician at
a state university doesn't rank that high in the world,
probably never contributed anything eternal,
just taught some other half-assed scholars,
got laid a little,
saw things totally clearly,
wrote some clear formulas
on the chalk board for the janitor to erase.

Heavy Metal Mike

Man, that was when
(over undo proto meaning)

Mike got substantial as
the leaves were just

turning into elevators common
cracked perception Mike

got windy or more likely
I was trying to be homeless

again or perish dually Mike
liked being an animal too much

because of something
to do with his serious headphones

when he blew something off
some guy was upstairs in his room

and Mike was smoking a love
cigarette downstairs with me all

shit all over the table CDs alchemy
books objects how did he get those

expensive fags correctly man the
guy's upstairs

and Mike portends I'm now self-employed
quite rigid and designed of

oracular say not Mike
Visene bubblegum tacs and taco shells

I'm so sorry I was late shall disorder
my mental problem life

Mike was saying I'd
take acid every time I could I've

never ever had a bad trip he's
got those big headphones his usual

rambling gait the old women
loved and never suspected my grandma

he hung paper took her wallet fought
fake combat and got jacked

over a phenomenally huge bag of bud
by yet another bunch of punks

with crazy crooked teeth and dirty fingers
can play fully two chords

on rolling guitars that mirror
inane serenity cops coughing

badges exploding patriarchy willowing
my name's Mike I'm everything

and I'm enjoying it
memory not enjoining taken together

if you follow these strange rudiments
you will see him

on a prospect of hip-hop metal melodies
because I'm a christian that's

why they want me I can't help
it dude if I love the devil

because he's beautiful he's a fallen angel
like me I'm here to help tomorrow

I'm gonna sign a million dollar deal
I'm suing St. Mary's they kept my sweater

don't fuck with me I'll sue
your fucking ass

the writer of this poem saw Mike oh
fuck final eviction notice with

what appeared
to be a hot young girl with a car

and a little money all instinct and lips
we animal or rolled cigarettes

black art photo maintenance ECT
the truth over all is

if you go in sane you'll come out crazy
if you go in crazy you got half a chance

but in Mike's immense capability of missupposition,
or dancing, or

half saying the dreary and
bright decay of the blind eye

like he found Superman's address
like evolution subsumed to just this

like some guy is in your
room for just this, playing

the shitty guitar, the
guy's got crooked teeth and yellow

fingers (granted, like me)
and leads Mike blind

to the tobacconist, they how
in the hell

prime and foretaste of dove
religiously mirror comicbook

creeps who haven't showered in a week
but eclipse the naked fervor

nothing to do no words no
angels under the corrupted sun defy

big Mike and his backpack
running another errand for a

buck right about
ready to sleep on a heating thing

you know, a bunch of bums
who got everything they need

Metal Metal Metal
I work for Homeland Security

and just got promoted
because yeah Obama fucking called me

and I am a Christian
it's right here I only got laid

once and it was
the absolute worst experience of my life

because my chakras are
fucked up they taught me in

the hospital I can get any
woman I want 'cus I know

the laws of attraction we were gonna
fuck but the orderly came in

do you hear my spinning do you
have you met me before

I just got outta lockdown
Mike said

and Mike walked and walked
in the Shadow of the Snowman

and the streets became his song
and the lilt became his pavement

I can't act I know the structure
Mike keeps it down

how many cigarettes will it take
dead cigarettes, words you've never heard

Mike say must recourse, a blind
Transylvanian hooker with braces

waitress at Blueberry Hill Chuck Berry
Mike gets free food wondering

and Christ come down some guy he
met for five seconds is his new

roadie cops on suspicion alone stories
you'll not exactly piece together

you won't hear this again about
Mike staring through the

sun after contemplating rolling papers
and a girl at the gas station

saying Jesus is inside me but even
splintered ideas propound heaven

I'm calling Brown and Croupen tomorrow
can you give me a cigarette

thank You Father for the end of sex
and the soft moon, the sun's explosion

the kids I don't think will ever feel
in front of the screen the

girl's with the oh he's hot, he's hot
the ape-like certitudes and twisted

revision of reference apply until you're
at some waste party and

everyone is fucking everyone without
beauty, without the slightest word

so sex ends, so green becomes green,
so gloves become bandages, so ghosts become grunts

and gaffes over girls one likes
in teeming mental trysts of

embarrassed abstraction, petty
drunken rumors, Mike bounced,

Mike borrowing a five with glassy eyes
near to having escaped the street

and back again, his I'll live here forever,
my stepdad is fucked up on

I want to be a Christian
but I read the temptation bible

and I tithe, that's my consideration
I want to have sex but I'll say I'm small

my fucked-up chakra system is all out of whack
when they elect me in 2024 you

better believe it because they taught
me in the hospital

the laws of attraction if
I am willing to leave a woman behind

so fuck them at Cicero's ("I'm looking
for a frontman, dude") my

mom won't give me my
drums back but I should shred on the guitar

I don't fuckin care I've heard enough and
you better start listening to me

I talked to them in the office they
gave me another month but I don't

care like the song says I'm worthless
man I can fuckin survive on the streets

I know how to a guy asks me for a
cigarette I say sure fifty cents

and I know the laws of attraction and
Prometheus Rising this shit has been

passed down don't worry about me
I'll see you at the drum circle

I hate the people in this building
anyway the secrets of

the universe are in my mind but
no one wants to listen to me I

told them I needed an Ativan shot
but my doctor wouldn't admit me

he's French fuckin smart man and
I know him dude

so half this shit is to even me out I
know I smoked a bowl two days ago

I fuckin admit it man can I put
a couple of shirts and pants in your laundry

he really did look good in a way
I went back some, I thought

on some level he might be totally on,
meet some great rich girl and a producer

where's he now, recording his comeback,
bigger, volatile, willing to spill all the secrets.

Pass

it was never like this
the birds in their hardscrabble way
did they really perceive the sun
did they smell the juniper

we've looked down on their fluttering
from our mute resolute sky
and never heard their sense or knew
if they flew where they had to fly

and I with my morose book at a bar
short of breath Hope's rose hand on his
back he begins to drift and fall
to where there are no crying birds at all

Reading Sonnet

I tried to have my eyes in such a way
would demonstrate behind the podium
a not-so-meretricious double, say
the manner pollen comes from petals flung

or birds a-twitter on telephone lines,
layers of ease we use to guile a past
encumbered, and not getting back from wines
to bottles or to grapes; I spoke; then fast

along the audience I heard a voice
as soft, but still I heard it whisper "work";
I whispered my "reality", my choice
to deal, I guess, where signs and ways have forked.

And coming up I found my tongue had cleft:
I picked up my embarrassed book and left.

Ass-Kicking, Delivered at Blueberry Hill

Down in the dank Red
Sea bar swaying to
rank reggae we ran out
of cash so I crossed the

street to Blueberry Hill to use
the ATM and weaving
through the crowd three
sultry and swarthy guys in

metro shirts and Wash U coats
made the mistake of snickering
about me and my chosen multi-
colored scarf so I took

them 5'3" and 130 each and
grabbed their necks and pounded
their heads into the glass and I
got stars turned into my teeth

as I whipped around my tongue
and right-handed proverbs a
stupid fake indie rock scumbag
with his bright cell on my girlfriend's

number he stole I was once
while I hit upon a girl outside
the bathroom perforce I drove
him there to Tiresias and while

the blood gathered and the women
moved I taught the kind of phallus

that contends with finality,
abrupts all the absences,

and the cops can't catch me—
I'm completely dead to the law,
I've been delivered into orality,
I'm a spectre between the lips.

Promo

I'm tired of the magick and
I certainly can't tell
what's hell anymore but I
think it might have something
to do with our strange goodbyes
and my listing at
last from Dole to Obama
and your terrible groping for
the phone in the light, I
charge the nothing-without-angst,
the innocence of the persecution birds,
the menace of the midnight pillows;

when I come up all dismasted
and trying to replicate the garden word
I think somewhere it might
be easier to let
the genitals remain riddled and unnamed,
the ribbons twisted, the rhymes profane,
I think when we part without sex
your reaching couplets are to blame—but
I've had it! Delineating these
delusions is all that remains:
you, you're a witch.
And I'm the literary Jesse James.

Vampires

Wherever she is I swear
  I will turn her off,
  cast my downward eye
at the Walgreen's aisle
  and let out my soft
  vitriolic mumble.

(or cast upon the long earth
  of Mike's party,
  1538 Wecheli Lane,
  Andrea Divus was there,
and as I turned with torn pants
to throw my 15 cent soda in the trash
  I thought I saw her eyes flash
  and light those darkened lips
  she licked while glancing at my
  yellow fingertips—all I could
ever know about it was ancient, ancient)

So scoff, you base lovers, scoff,
  and bite at my bloody words:
  give me six strings
  and three chords
and I swear I will turn you off.

What People Think

It feels so good to be cold now,
beautiful and frozen,
easier to walk with one's head up,
easier to sit by the fountain
and unburden oneself of a dime—

even if that wish is for fire.

Brevity on Broadway

You and your reference and your black hair and
dress caught me there on Broadway '96

as I was gallantly carrying twelve roses
for my blonde girl, come out of some bar

and you were there bent tending to a strap
on your heels and that beautiful fabric

coming up high and your eyes were smiling
and you curiously asked the time my condition

wound up as I was to glimpse another subject
this is coming out all love and clarity

but when you saw those flowers and my
demeanor like a boy from the apocrypha

who would rather throw a guitar onto the
subway track than sit through Berlioz

one classy dame as they might say all red lips
and dark wisps I fumble and resist

there in '96 when you somehow blessed me and I forget:
for whom were those great big flowers anyhow?

Oceans Can Belong

Bone weary, frustrated
beyond belief, the
oppressed alcoholic says,

"if oceans can belong so can we."

So I lay my guitar
across the Metrolink tracks
and consider the evening breeze.

"If oceans are wrong then so are we."

What was meant not to be found
has been found
and purchased. Right around
the curve of Lesbia's waist. Right
around her oval face and scars.
Thank God for blackouts, thinks
the oppressed alcoholic, what would
I do without these little stars, without
these aboriginal phrases.

"If oceans are songs then so are we."

No Sleep Until Sauget (for Amanda G.)

Staked and screeching into the daylight,
hammered by dawn, the endless
door closing behind me and the bouncers weeping
for the troops—oft in these haunts have
I made an ass of myself—the lotus
are wearing thin and the cross is still cool,
omnirepressed and soothsaying as I am
having hit rush hour on 40 in a cab
and turning to the dorky dancer beside me
and saying if you remember
what it's like as free then
tear down the walls that haunt your
liberty, do not mark upon the body,
living forever seems more and more likely,
I hurriedly jump out at SLU and suddenly
up Grand I get a taco and sit by the fountain
and wait for clarity to come in the form
of the Otherness of my own blood, flying, eyes wide
but only askance and sly so I hit Jesuit Hall
and ask for an exorcist, a bunch of priests drag
me across the street, door closing behind me,
bleached and staring at the sun, not
exactly organized or covert for that matter,
all of this coming from the experience of looking
into a cruel mirror and getting blood drawn
without a bandaid among heroic whisperings,
I'm left there on Lindell and love
at least a particular, or the generalization
of oh Orpheus I promise not to turn
around for you and the Maenads I'm
sorry I wouldn't sleep with you and Apollo
thank you for the light and the walls

are surely coming down now I'm becoming part
of the air, it's the ultimate walk of shame,
what sensitivity and surprise, what defeat,
what density and petechiae, what tenses,
to become completely true and all read through.

ABSENT

Barroom Veteran

It's hard to perceive things, you
know, when you've got
a heart-shaped hole in your heart

and it's hard to lie, you
know, when you've got
the truth all along your part

and yet it's hard to tell the truth, you
know, when disaster
is your only art

so it's hard to be comforted, you
know, when your hands
can't pull the curtain apart

and you can't be reached, you
know, because
the fabric is so thick and dark

and what separates you, you
know, is a tiny element that
makes a shuddering spark

that lights the objects, you
know, that you do
not know and cannot take apart

and now you breathe, you
know, while she passes
by and doesn't hear, you lark.

Piss Poor Parenting

I always thought there was something
I was missing,
the joint in the park and
the heaviness of the sigh;

wondering just won't do it anymore.
So I talk to a friend who hates me
over the fence and I notice
when he comes back the book
I'm reading lights up
and his directions are changing.
Didn't I cut a gallant charm?
Wasn't I sad and beautiful?

To be sex-starved, star-quilted,
waving goodbye
to the fascinated
blackness where he was,
he and his
intelligent girls with nipples
showing, exactly where we are not,
unutterably and out of control,
the budding but today
irreparable, cutting the sky,
anxious about not being anxious,
the lowdown on language,
"I am changing the weather,"
"this has been written,"
"my bathos of beatitudes,"
under the power he wants to deal,

no more coinage, the
devil got me from behind,

the admissions councilors and human resources
stained glass leaving
belated or ill-formed discontinuity,
tears all doorstep long,

please say I'm not turning into Bukowski
please tell these exciting heroin addicts
  I dreamt I wasn't French
please say Belz said I sweat like Orson Welles
please thank my buddy Sean for waking me up
  out of a drunk sleep in my car on the parking
  lot so I could take the ACT
please thank God for my expulsion
please say these poems are not about nothing

The Return to Repression

We looked like each other from the start—the
caterwauling glance and the
lesion in the "devil made me
smoke it" consciousness—

so naturally I rubbed my hand through my hair
and left my Aunts and coffee
and met you in the stacks;
if sadness were a more accurate view of the world,
mom I'm home late mom,
it wouldn't have been the brain that
got us into that summer dress, it wouldn't
have been just
Mozart who wanted to
tell us all about himself on the ceiling.

Oh, I couldn't live without it, I
couldn't hate the cops, I couldn't
derive images of resolution, I
couldn't abstract angst and expiation,
I couldn't blow up new notions of freedom—

it was a very humbling night indeed. After
you flew I got hit with a heavy bum assault
at my HUD building, I became
bored with all the
same old visions and procrastinations
and took my
money I mean medicine,
and nearly returned.

You, you saw my cleavings grow into
their disinheritance of clarity,

the sea of books again from both worlds
we stepped
and good halting conversation
that meanders or hints we hated
about as much as possible,

you know the world is my idea and shit

but did not work in the sense of flower
and lovely lingering days
or stank but somnolent senseless
turned fruition I stopped coughing back at
the eternal readings, revisions,

could I be getting close? Still miles to go.
My sister says I'm better than Rimbaud.

Anhedonia as the Letter W

Surprised to find himself still human
and failing to see
himself on television amidst the
kissing lovers he could never
speak like that, he awoke
sitting on a cold hard floor
with a bunch of broken glass
that he could not piece together to
make a window of ideas, how he
used to talk about the soul was
whatever that was, and the glass was sharp,
and if he found out about a hot
Christian girl he wouldn't have
freaked out on the bus and said
I'm the Other I'm just like you
but I'm not you can't
treat me like an Other I contain
myself I'm not some Other I
define myself by Otherness hey
dude I'm the Other we do things
differently by this privilege we're
all deep down the same
why do you know I'm just like
you [from the editor: Nota Bene:
Matt Freeman doesn't revise shit]
and physical longing and length
that revert to a language of ideas
in the rose or windblows
of clever particularities, of time,
Mr Wordsworth running around
with his pure sister and fake wood
and false glass and distance why
we here are here transformed he

awoke to find was possibly not as unpleasant
as he had previously thought—
and he said again he was the Other
and by this stance was expected
to claim that people were basically birds
and wings were words
and that it is possible to die of salvation,
and that it is possible to die of strength,
of difference, of meaning, of totality,
and that it is only ineluctable
that one day one should hear his own voice
echoing in a empty trashcan:
"I could never hold her hand like that."

To the Other Side

I look at Morrison in the corner
we're all getting high
there's a hot girl between us
she's wearing very short jean shorts
she's Lesbia with her imprecations
of falsity and I feel so sorry for
Jim because of his tepid psychotic leanings
that never got him all the way there
and he asks if I'm fucking with him
or am I some kind of gay dude then
he turns to Lesbia
crossing and uncrossing her legs so cool
and he tells her
you've got that aura of election upon you
their eyes meet so latent and bizarre
because I know what Morrison's thinking:
"the given; and a girl in Autumn.
strange rebukes from her Siren eyes.
Seven miles to the temple.
I hear it so clearly, what she says."

Just this once, just this once, the
voodoo of the too-long look tripped up.
Later, in bed, Lesbia comes clean to me:
"I was thinking of buying some running shoes."

Morons, Getting Wasted

As I went to sleep I dreamed of pink
and that permeated my voice
in a fluttering that laid me down
and I was as bare as a bird that
pink soft curtains and pink carpet
and even Christ pink too I took
from my famous near-visions
of hell but pink landscape
now I lived in pink
and but that pink adult mobile that
lived over me and suffused
me that I almost regained everything
but loud bells and alarums
or pink monks and gadgets and make-up sex
I came to and fro
so I had this party to go to
nervous after my pink nap Denise
pulls up in the SUV
after me downstairs for fifteen minutes
smoking lost cigarettes and I get in her car
and there's Denise with a patterned pink
skirt and pink coat I'm going
to run back to Apollo until
my feet bleed daylight pink daylight I
only tell you this to find pink—the cops
didn't hide the dope—the stoners did—and it was pink—

Finally Get Born

You coughed 'cus I coughed you motherfucker
right around the time I saw a dress explode
when I biked toward Haven, I wasn't dreaming

finally I'm getting more and more emotional
and even feel the trees breathe with me
but it's not cosmic or anything, it can be explained

or if you look deeply into the bare television
if sparks the right ideas are coming closer
I, whatever was forgotten purely solidified again

moving toward the streetlamp saying not the moon again
a dreary releasing possessive, peerless white wrists,
getting laid unconsciously, greatly concept perception

if you'd like to tell me about movements and fragments
someday I will reveal part of my history with the police
and the old nutmeg about standing in the corner of Boo
     Radley's

when T Bone threw me up against the wall outside after
having had 24 shots and said he wasn't gay
that impact hallucinations make weird rent

to the farthest quotidian ever almost possible in thought
philosophers of history never have insane toothaches
Demeter never had what you would call a clean womb

so what if shit makes no sense to you but bathos
or you believe you have suddenly a high unusual amount of
     energy
trust me, trust me, the moon lies all the time

Six Months on the Chain Gang

The wind in the trees but not for
me the object, the object, oh shit
the object as I turn
to escape Lindell with my new C harp
and land in Terra Haute
like Lesbia says I sound
like I have a destitute angel in
my pocket
I wrist and forfeit order
to the flippant cops—each regret
is a new note, a Greyhound ribbon,
I'm down to two rolled cigarettes—and
if it weren't for the leaves
I would never have learned how to
cry the gaze and bus station mirror
and the bottle slide,
the pregnant woman with her sad luggage
looks at me while I fuse
the bluesy accoutrements of the lowdown
but I don't know anything I affect
Oh lesbia and the bent
note now I will address you lovers
you leavings you heightenings
you roses to be plucked until you wither:
the jailhouse ain't no plaything
believe me it ain't no lie.

Cascado for Hope and Amanda

It's so easy to know more about water than me,
and yet that night my bed
gave up its fullness and
after I thought I saw Hope again at Shell
the flower of contempt began to lose its petals
and as the ocean came out of the TV
I was alone on some
electric wave I knew no one would ever believe—that's
part of what I bear—
and I came up and down and across then
I knew I valued
being normal way above everything else like
someone would who woke up to an oceanic sense
but that was back when I felt
like I was falling, like I was about to be saved,
back when I used to put
a flower of mercy in my window
that never lacked for water and I
went up to Hope at Shell
like a cat with a dead-bird origin
impossibly explaining my pipe dreams
of power and Hope turned away
to the electric gas pump voice outside
which would
give me the key to access my own bed
to read Psalms in the attic while water dripped
because it has become so
difficult for me to enter the very little Other
bottlewater hippies on the bus are
saying I'm not all that referential
so that the Perrier freaks carry me to the cross
think big they say in your
Gaelic water regret and fierce Tutonic streams

or English blonde girl on the Thames
I can't turn over just remain feminine and prone
I brought you a canoe like this dream
walking with Amanda unreal up Skinker
too thin from being expatiated a
young man in a dry mouth
gaping, paused at the wet faces on the metro,
my friend the dick-out newspaper delivery guy
the world, the numinous nothing, the
horror and acrimony of forgiveness, blatant time,
I knew that Orpheus knew that sex was an
abnormal waste of consciousness, they killed him, I
got sober, came clean about turning into a vampire,
Oh there's Hope, she prepared the ablution,
I kick off the sheets, everything's perfect in the necromedia.

The Most Hated Poet in St. Louis

People are always asking about my defeats
and the aura of election hangin' over my head
twelve bushels, twelve stars, twelve palm leaves

so how about "wake up you son of a bitch"
my father cried I blurily saw him at my
door and raised my head out of the puke

and saw my puke pillow and focused more
to see the puke on my guitar and notebooks
when he grabbed me by the neck through

the sunday kitchen and bacon outside
there were ferns and branches on my car
old '76 and a big yellow streak

and I had another dream about resentment
and double intuition last night burned free
and Mystery, western as can be in her blonde

disguise, said I was better than Delphi,
and that if I embraced her nothing would come
of it because I fucked up with regard

to righteousness, the moral dot
in the middle of a cynical spiral that
cuts through Lot with salt and I

said you dumb defects I was born free
what women don't want this intellectuality
she mailed a cryptic letter to the FBI

now I did not kiss her at the traffic light
and (I) alone in my sweaty scarf
cannot prove that St. Louis is not Athens

one must get one's priorities evened out
nonetheless Tim how did I get home Oh I
followed you for a while your head was down

in the passenger's seat I figured if you made
it that far you'd make it home and (I) alone
remember the four causes and the currents

and the squares especially, the great aporia
that would solidify and then pass, the names,
the superstructure that would soak these tarts.

I Was All that Was Left of the World

My apology is in this poem:
I threw my keys into the forest
and a little later on my wallet
beginning everything with me
so that I could not be identified finally
eating rice hungrily stooped over
lengthily free of guilt
in a ninth street shop
caring not while everyone watched, ME,
pulling my hair out.

(I couldn't get a ride to the airport)

I'd e-mailed the end regrets
from ground zero in the computer lab
as it began to rain
wearing a rain coat
while waiting on the rain
and looking at stanzas upon the screen.

I'm going back to the city
where I won't be known,
where you can go bleeding into the hospital
and be stitched without shame.

(I am becoming an athlete again,
a child whose strength is running on
future identity)

Thoughts

I guess it would be the -us
not the -um because if
you think about it it is a guy
but on the other hand the guy
in his present state would be
neutered, I guess, sort of, so
in that case maybe it would be
the -um knowing it's gotta be either
the -um or the -us because in
either case the plural is castrati
definitely not taking the feminine -ae
but 'castrati' is possibly not
a Latin word at all, possibly it's
Italian and then, I'm thinking,
it would be the -o ending, right?

It's absurd anyway to think
about such things, don't do
anything, stay still, someone will
walk through that door and everything
will be all right—but,
wait, people are the problem, no,
you're the problem. NO, the question
is what to do next. "In my opinion ... "
You ought to ... in any case ...
"Breathing is good." (You've learned
that, finally) (he thought; who
is 'he'?) Spiral is a good metaphor
to use when you finally get all
this down but don't be too blunt
(like the horrible blunt edge etc.

Opposing Transference

The greatest compliment I ever got
occurred in the emergency room
of Barnes-Jewish when I was 27
after I'd explained that
a) I'd been born breech there in '73
 and
b) I'd discovered I was
 1. Jewish
 2. Part Black
 and
then picked up my copy of Harold Bloom's
greatest criticism
beginning to read
while moving each of my
extremities
to completely different rhythms.

A beautiful young doctor
walking by said,
"There's Freeman,

 turning it on from the start ..."

Amen, sweetheart.

Progress

It's not enough to be a bum
or gay for pay

or to rip out the shrubs at a movie
theater and race from the parking lot
as the cops come in infatuated—

oh, it's not nearly enough to
stand at the precipice of a
gaping wound and decide to
go in and wound yourself and carry
along all that you love and try
not letting it go
as you fallout and away into
the clouds that are above the earth
and backwards for the incarnation downward
into the sibling wounds what

would be enough
can't say but crazy lights tonight
while I repress this pen and only
know whatever's repressed returns
and foolish me:

I should've dug ditches for hundreds of dollars.

"Gay for Pay"

Matchless here in no man's land, can't
seem to breathe, the
wind goes right through me as
I wait for the holes in my coat

and I'm a petty criminal, bounced for my
strange accent, girls looking me up and down,
I follow the curve in the track
I stop off for some honeysuckle and sex

that conjuring machine
that capable wizard

I can't remember how I came this far
when I settled at the counter
and acted corrupt in Joplin just
outa jail I said she
didn't write all of her songs and a guy
in camo overalls sneered through his
coffee and said he screwed his sister but
I couldn't catch the antecedent—

this far, so far from correct, I'm the one who
drew the lines between the stars so
long ago and figured they were random,
and now this wind and rain and the sun right through me.

Maudit

Nobody believed I was the last boy on earth
—they didn't believe I'd been drowning either—when
I came to the swingset
out the murmuring wooded area comments
about my long blonde hair some
mother complained I was a girl but
I had this weird grey protection
I still use that was slightly lighter
if I needed to take my backpack to the library
but back then I could smell the oak
or endings not known, it's been twelve
confused mothers now for centuries I
keep running over brooks then that was sweet
when I touched something
you knew right away that I had
touched it because of my colored eyes
and ocean and zeal I knew then
when an adult was smoking a joint
laughing at my salesman father all big
and surviving on commissions no one could do
vocal thievings parameters scalding red hot
I've known for years that was genius
but now on cobblestone
some guy with a joint I've fought
for eleven years tied to bandana girls what
perforce poet came back and did not get laid
even samurai mental college teeth but I
was young, little, astounded, I
sat and did nothing but a big fire I
go now by these crazy guitars
and knowledge they can seriously kiss
it I had to sacrifice just all overt
intoxication, symbolic heavy on me,

dad salesman dying with no furnace
got off the bus driver's saying he's got
pimp juice and sober performance anxiety
he needs must be loved or else
when the Imaginary hit him in
High School he washed cars
and lunched with Father Ong tearing
out hi verbal territory before it
was clear who was saying what because
these ashcan artists never rode the blues buses
tin sufferings and aluminum paper prophecies
and as usual God prefers the second chance
so discharged dad dismayed he
went to the tallest building possible
becoming instant aggrandized fluid
the never-hip hip salesman not unseen
for my pleasant churches God there
new windrows and duck blinds across
the wooded want and the sacred chapels
raindrops on future broken windshields
   the times they make no sense
Phoebe sacrifice into the quotidian
loud father of the burnt bulb phase
I tried walking around
without for less than a day the end
he mentioned in his application
he'd been the last boy on earth
and had stolen everything that got rained on
and that loneliness was sweet
and that he always used to rhyme—
he left out the drowning part though
being too aware that that was fabulous—and
that he had
taken long crazy walks to blues bars
or tried
to sell his sister on the fact that he was Jesus

but none of that really mattered
when I got down
to the nuts and bolts of the greatest
reaction formation in history plus
something like atypical mountain
built on last resorts assume, he thought,
that everyone but me is totally high
  you've got a nice smile (and
  now our friendship is ruined)
and I came without feeling out of the water
not two-layered but two-doved, two-fired
I don't remember having awakened
but I knew that I liked it most
right before I was thrown in it
was like having a check for a million
dollars but nobody would cash it,
chains on my ankles, a guy named
'moochie' blinding my shoulder I say
I have nothing but similitude now,
the guys with the tie-dye seem so slow,
I'm hammering away at the dawn,
I'm outrunning all the alien eggheads—Oh
there's a whispering
and a superior coughing, I can't
accept anything without a dull longing
and a vacant placement
so I grab at my own lapels and shake
shake the girl in me and the guy from hell—remember
when you were at that mirror
and cell after cell dismembered
and you were haunted by hoodlums
and laughing hatred broke your ribs;
now take your trophy and pawn it—you
won't need it where you're going.

Hobo Repression Blues

OK, I've said my thirteen last words
on insolubility
and had my vinegar—
now you can teach me what a kiss is.

And I don't like to brag but
I've slid down the
rainbow of hell and
landed on my own idleness.

My sex is a creepy shroud.
My paradox can be dealt in numbers:
so if I should perhaps oh   boy relent
I'm one who's been in mental prison pent.

(though if you saw me walking on
I might create an already broken rule
that blanks the street with perfect words
and says one bush is worth a thousand birds)

This artifice is a wall of tongues and skin
deep structure would negate; don't
worry too much about me. I've got nothing.
Look at big Matt. He used to be a hero.

After the Praecox

After walking down the road
for a while bleached in the light
everything began to look the same.

So I went up the hill before the tracks
and scraped my knees upon the little
rocks and glass and sat upon the ties.

Birds on the wire, black and red,
made claims I could not understand;
they left me in the heat, the cold.

As I was, I wasn't quite alone: I
mistook ten passing freight cars to
diagnose me for my Danville girl

I'll marry down the road, when
time comes jointed back again, and
put my yellow hands throughout her

hair, and put my cheek upon her
pillow, and have myself what passing means:
the flattest bottom in fourteen dreams.

Senses

The first thing I died today
was awake to discord,
books coming off shelves
and girlfriends not answering phones,
diffuse coffee in the scattered light.

And have I known hatred like a politician,
seen the burning eyes of a saint on my sleep,
troubled by the black and white of things,
insisting on the stabbing aural and scopic.

My hands cannot feel where they grope sometimes
and are pestered by the graphs
in their own memories; because
once harmony
harbored in their grasp.

Still things are shaping themselves into
eruptions in my room tonight.
I will lie down to senses, I will
hang my white shirt over the TV,
I will try to calculate the organizations
of two beauties that bring another.

Some Words

You know damn well at this point,
nowadays,
if a Nazi came knocking on your door
you'd be all thinking,
"Either I'm going to call the police
or tell this guy off or something ...
possibly I will kick his ass."

But that's not how it was years ago
in Germany. You know,
I mean you must know,
that people used to see Nazis
walking down the street and say,
"Those Nazis are great."
And you know damn well it was that way
or the Nazis would've never taken power.

Where, exactly, am I going with this?

I'm thinking of the words 'psychosis,'
'psychotic' and 'psycho.' What do these
words mean? Are they dangerous words?
What do they have to do with Nazis?

I just remember finally being set free,
being set free, from the barrier in my head—the
ability to laugh, the ability to cry
came back to me, but I was too nervous and
had to go to the hospital, where I walked and walked
pacing, and talked, finally talked and for days
I refused to take any kind of medicine
but I could not sleep, I could not sleep, and
I was too happy, and I was too sad, voices too,

and they finally coerced me into taking the pill.

I stood near the pharmacist with it in my hand.

I swallowed it with a little water
from the cup.
I handed the cup back empty.
"So, what kind of medicine is this?"

"Anti-psychotic."

Have you ever seen a heart drop? Have you ever
seen a face immediately pale?

I don't know why I'm writing this,
it's too embarrassing. Amen.

FINISHED

3rd Song, New Dorm

So Father help me I decided
to try swimming
and in the deep end as always
two girls of terror:

"So I'm waiting for him to try
taking it to the next level."

"What's his name again?"

"MATTHEW."

Oh shit, I should have literally stayed
in the shallow
end with the new mothers, the young
mothers who if I run
up to them panting saying
I finally figured
it out I am definitely John the Baptist
they will not call a firetruck—

and I stepped out of the water and I
went back to my wooden room
fully expecting a dove to appear at my window
but instead Lesbia was in my bed
and at my back was a world of steel.

Amanda Laughing

Sometimes when things are real not
real, like handcuffs, like
monstrous repressions,

when I cannot be defeated
again or listen closely
to the given and
desperate songs once I turned
and Amanda
in some guy's green Corvette
flew past and laughed
because I might have been big and sincere

and surrendered up dope and credit cards
but mysteriously potent
including heart attacks, left brains,

answers to questions not asked—performed
in the utmost circumstance—come
drive by my building and scream:
I promise not to confide, I'll go further ...

of course, things are blurry and sane and
I could always be wrong, yes,
I could always be wrong.

It Makes Me Wanna Puke

I say I will not stand for shitty poems
but there I am in the hallway
of the hotel with another
protesting
I will not kiss on the lips

then my teeth next to the vase
it's easier and pink in the dark
paisley carpet on my socks
he wants to hit the ATM
but Carl's on the beeper
and the threat of that because
I know too well how it feels to
have a red face and no rent

(there was a college kid once
we did it on a stoop but we
had to go up for cab money from
his roommate and I saw the
titles on his shelf I recognized
but too poor then drink it up
back at Carl's the minute I
crossed the threshold
the heaviness hit me like a feather
and I took off my glasses in
order not to see the crumbs on the floor)

so maybe I ought to put on some wig
go to the steakhouse crevice
with the scotch drinkers breath
credit cards Langston Hughes was born here
but nothing matters the poets call fancy
fifteen years later at Carl's I wake

to find myself pissing on the kitchen
floor dead letters
the room's just a little smaller

Hard Times Lounge

Resisting the downpour, drenched
in mercy under the cardboard
hotel on Market, watching
the wrenching wrens with
half a can a coke and
only straw for tobacco

I whisper here comes the mayor
of Munchausen between
the torch and quarter moon—but
this time he has to quarrel

with what all these years have done
to me, me and my regretful
guitar and rancid maple,

before he goes up to his hotplate.
I see him just the same and I

think to myself
this just might be it, forever,

I really might start to levitate
any moment now—

Hard Times and Bathsheba

Paradise was waiting to mess me up again
with its breasts and oblivion
and even though I thought
and I thought the streetlights were
tendering me a system or that
Bathsheba's silver rings
shone on a part of a grand revision
there was really no technical
reason for me to stay and on
my way I told
the security lady "I hide what
I hide" which would all be revealed
immortal after an epic journey
looking for a payphone—to call
Bathsheba, down to
the Mississippi in seventeen degrees
singing Mother I didn't go into this
writing poor words on the wall for
just anyone could see
the drift of the lines we try to impose
inherent in the death of meds
perhaps you call yourself Good Luck
to beautiful paupers
who must see the mirror's fair face
I exactly doubted hell then rode along
and saw my very own heightened collapse
and it took my breath away, I
tried to feel myself, I tried
to sort through all this messed-up yarn
and find my viscera, like repeatedly
trying to break out
of prison for no reason but
the ghost of being English about everything

excuse me will I say
when I find a
fucking payphone and call Bathsheba
and beg her to listen just once more
to the emasculating ambivalent freakout
and empty symbols with no purpose
I put a shroud over my DVD
and a rose in my army helmet
knowing all along that our
stars are our selves, burn away
all the snarky and stupid bits and
tell Bathsheba that I want to
hold her pulse and safety sex, that
I would retire these scribbled-on boots,
that I could create a sail, that
I could heart this coming rain of identity
something love, and else, a payphone

little piece of cornbread layin on the shelf.
You want anymore? You can sing it yourself.

Discourse of the Delmar Hysteric

After I used a perfect pencil
I found I had to
pick up from the parking
lot or else to punch a
bunch of holes in tires
outside the back of Fitz's
for no reason
other than a necessary divorce
I am the reality fish Bishop let go
my name written nowhere shame
I saw a woman so proud of her man
sitting on a bench while he
and a buddy talked about motors
"and if there's no fluid it
steel on steel and peters
out you must lube
and pump it up" she beamed
at his steady eyes and comeback
big tattoos love the
disguise that varicates the clearest
things in life my penetration
into the uncanny detail
above the verdure vacuum
I tortured, hook-befallen,
marked, spoken, seasoned,
crested, big-moneyed, found
in the waves, harder than a sentence.

"Oh Narrow is the Way"

There was a guy in Latin class (with
fangs) who was normal
and calm and once he with the
contemporary shaggy hair had
me come over and do bong hits

during (insane) a very placid baseball game

suddenly my mind came up and shrieked
so we got in his car to hit a
bar and bring me down (loud)

but at the light these Asian girls
behind us in a Ford
quite convenient were going to kill us
so I hopped out
at the light and started running
finally cooled down at the corner so
my buddy pulled up and I got back
in I was behind words
and beyond putting this force
into a tight structure

who behind us now but a hoosier in a beat old
truck—they had switched somehow—
I got out again and broke all the way
to my apartment tried
to hide locked door and bounced on
my bed meanwhile these people
convened in the hall laughing

'cus now I remembered I had
yes talked to that girl

and on the way to
the next bar made some
strange semaphore the sad
hippie had tested me and bummed a smoke
the windows were too tight I got up and
ran—no one was there in the hall—
to that guy's house he was home with the bong
I asked him if I could get an eighth
(I had to make it right) but

after what just happened, he said,
after what just happened?

Mooching for Two

Phoebe, there's a blackness coming over me.
I tried listening to the windrows,
I heeded the highest advice,
I put under what seemed to be surfacing—

then the words appeared like
little diamonds and cut me up;
I'm bleeding from astral interpenetration.

They say that it's probably true that
I was barely able to buy a tin can of beans
and put them in the
microwave while I was playing
my lute, the specifics indeed voluminous
and watch myself with the hard
rain and exhaust the peculiarities
I stepped as if Orpheus into triage
you patterned and you yourself you
still had on your own hospital bracelet
and I keep forgetting and can't do kids right now
my voice is still cracking and tore up
at mastering the vast violations it
takes to be absolutely chained to the sea:

Phoebe ... just whose mother are you?

You Might be a Schizophrenic

If you're getting a pack of
cigarettes at 4am you think
it might be thursday but
makes no sense it's not thursday
or the morning
and the cashier's vampire looks left
towards clouds and clouds
move so you go that way and
throw your jacket in the pond
and weary walk
back to the priests' dormitory
(talking over the talking
workshop facilitator laughing and
tell the admissions
lady you've got schizophrenia)
you might be a schizophrenic
or you meet a girl gossiping about that
girl in short shorts takes the pills
so you can't hear my thoughts
everything you know you tell her
don't make me cereal you poison
in a subsidized joint you try to lose
weight about benefits, fighting diabetes,
arguing over a dollar for ham and beans
and smoke bums bumming smokes
dealing with this under the sun she
says she wants an orgy never said
that because obviously my
parents got high before I was
conceived you might be a schizophrenic
that stairwell slipped and
hit every step with
your head fell off a swingset

beaten in Hell's Kitchen
ravaged upon Harold's Square
male nurse touches female nurse
you laugh and alone Mom signs you
out you payphone cried
if you recite ten medicines and doses
to various paramedics proudly
ain't getting it you might
be a schizophrenic chaos is not just a theory
first things, first causes,
fingerprints under the sun you might
if you think Dad's this glass and
Mom's this napkin and I'm the straw
because people in the attic told
me so and furthermore I am completely
normal you might be a schizophrenic
and if you finally get a date
and beforehand walk
to the store and walk
all around the store
thinking don't eat the garlic
don't eat the garlic it
will kill you and your
teeth are getting sharper
but no one notices you might
be a schizophrenic especially if your
date's an adventurous depressive
you can cheer each other up
you so rigid and can't believe someone
with long hair could be
homesick or someone with
pink hair could hold her boyfriend's hand
or that anyone
could exist without a gulf
and if something beautiful
surrounding the rain becomes horrific

and your buddies are all
in distress as if the salmon's gone
you live in terror of the phone
the sky itself repels clarity and
you burn like teeth the mistress
only performs in sleep but fake
you are in
the emergency room again and
recall your mom dyed her hair
therefore you are either
Jewish or a Nazi so that
when you get lonely you have
to close your eyes you might
be a schizophrenic and
finally it's your date and you
pick Lesbia up ten minutes
ago but can't be sure whether
you ate any garlic she has
a silver letter opener
disguised in her purse why me
why she was
looking in our journal obviously
by the way she
pronounced 'evening'
we leave the keys in the car
and the car running and
the doors open on Lindell and we believe
this might be love follow her up Grand
and they're closing in behind me
and I turn around to look there's
the big bridge, there's
the big bank and I might be
yes I certainly might be now

Dear Phone Company,

and I'm sorry I don't know you but I
if I have this fuzzy correctly (because
I bought a bag in
Springfield I'm not sure 1991 I
refuse to pay my bill and you know why
they planted my old buddy Gene
in the cops or not me
because I made a joke about him
because I have very few disciples
if you call me Paddy one more time
I kept Seamus
McDaniel's in business for six years
that I sculpted on my poor land line
mental schizophrenia
seven dollars a day to live on
the hospital said my genitals were in order
thank you Matt Blunt pittance corrupt
because I know merely
how to change everyone's sexuality
and read science like literature that's God
due to radios in the library
I am not like Ghandi
there, is, no, secret, knowledge,
I've, come, back, from,
the, phone, test, absolute,
finished, and, perfected,
Columbia, Missouri, Cops,
confound, me, persuasion,
I, resist, implantation—

Superhuman medication and Clozaril
I organize according to God
wants me through these blatant regions

of glass and crayon—
I'm a full-time scribbler, three quarters of a man,
now I know I've got your bug inside my hand.

I'm Normal, God Said

He always dreamed of
performing some heroic act
that would get him
a lot of glory and girls.

Through him went wildly
babies in bathtubs,
sorority girls in burning buildings,
guys on electric wires,
windy ships at sea where
he commandeered a lifeboat.

He always dreamed of saying goodbye
to a friend forever, and then
grabbing the gun of a gone-postal assailant.

But he always knew that meaning was deferred
under the dark wing of
hallucination, that deliverance
was garnered from getting entangled
with the ghost of the last girl who followed you.

Magdalene

Because one means everything, because
one is never young, never lonely, one
never looks into a crowded bar
from where it is cold outside,
because all one needs
is a systematic emblem of origins
that mouths and fractures the conversation,
because one feels a little too prepossessing
perhaps in toothpick jeans and
scraggily beard, burying everything
with the extreme caution of a non-conformist,
because one looks like a pretty little
anarchist from the suburbs and too much sex,
because one's car is too dirty and lips too pink,
because one's degrees are full of lies
and attempts in vain to reach the ceiling,
because one never gets quite behind
what is being said when it is noisy
and there is no sound whatsoever,
because one is always saying
things that are generally true, not in
order to get into one's pants,
for why would one want to do that,
because one is always coming off like
some kind of eunuch, listening
liberally ashen and unconscious to
the mute ruminations of lovers
one swears will not
make one one iota jealous, rigid,
because one balks at the
insane idea of putting one's penis into something,
because one suspects one can get through
to sex by an intense study of numerology,

because one's always got the feeling one's
been accused of some horrid crime
but cannot remember all of the details—

wait a second, I think that's her. I'll
only empty the ashtray and
take a sip of soda, ready to undo, ready
to outlay my peripheral utter, and
live between the innuendo of what's
just been said and what's been indicated.
The neutral can course itself in the smoke.

A Heartbeat from Homeless

I saw Mary Ellen again today
sitting with the guy who can't walk or talk
and they were holding hands
while they were looking away from each other
they were on the green couch
with the piss stain on it
and I walked into the light and stood there
thinking I would never
say I'm all about appearances
(guns don't kill people—the wind does)
and if I had struggled to get it back
I can recall speaking on the phone
in my timid mother's room
trying desperately to
remember how it was to be a boy
groping toward the more poisonous planes
so what if Mary Ellen goes down
Delmar picking up cigarette butts
seventy-one and doesn't know where she lives
but that smile—those bright eyes—
and the nothing with God or else
the nothing that is not
that makes some people hard and
some people soft—the saints and liars—
and I may not have known what it meant
but I knew that it was complete.

She Doesn't Like Me and There's a Tear in My Soda

I've been surrounded by birds tonight—it
was as if I were sitting
at an easel
invisible but for my tongue by the end of the bar
gesturing from a late acceptance,
creating clouds of even continuity
as dresses pooled at my stool
and I lightly held my brush
but instead of getting laid I got
trapped in a little elevator that
came down from somewhere I
might not exactly know or a phone booth
whose lines were cut, as
if I needed nothing but I was cut
they behaved as if I didn't even have a dick
should I shoulder my heavy wings
one came here, then another
they were touching each other with wide eyes
I must write
this down and send it
to the police I mean the principle elect
or I must hit on my mom I mean Mary
unless, of course, that is, perhaps
if she were someone I could bear losing barely—I
though I liked things the way they were—
as if my wet soda were a way back into meaning
or that time proves that
the nature of reality is fucked, some
inability of ours to submit to
priority, the despair of the dark
cloth woven into us as desire, the
electricity at the end of our fingers

that when we touch
we are dust together and
we wish we could go home
for they called me a fag a fairy a
frankenstein, and I had
all the will an acorn could have
when my skirt was torn from me
or my windbreaker, I am walking again
on Delmar I can taste the leaves
they put, the loneliness is quite clever
and the pin-drops are in my hand
and the west wind begs me to say
the epics are all over—
up Skinker in a thin coat
no hat and painful boots December—and
I only want
to lay back
with my head between your breasts
and feel the heat coming off your eyes,
from one little rock to the next
across the stream of reference—
the plotting birds, the bright
white yellow birds, the birds
all connected or not at nothing
we hammer against, their oh-so-light
feathers, and am I a gaunt old man
delivered into the Styx or Erebus I
cannot now know or the quotidian bricks
I hammer against or plurality—
there seems to be a whole lot of shit
going down that
these guys with stupid jackets don't know
about, shoulders high,
jutting mouths, breeders, dumbfucks
who don't need to think so
here I am

ringing bells against accusations
of indeterminate satisfactions, awakened
green by the bridge from man to woman,
the woman with teeth in
ruins and

  she doesn't like me
    she doesn't
like me she
    doesn't like me

and the turning birds in the gyre
of what's to become in the dark
we will not know of
fortune I shall say stupidly
with tremulous hands I steadily
but in a trance of beyond
sobriety stupid turn my face
to catch a tongue on my ear
to the left blonde birds then
my right dark nipples before
purple breasts I cannot
sing I shall forget Adam
I grape follow because remembered
time luckily out of stance
portray subjective labia
perhaps golden feathers casually
nothing care I chair see turn cause
cream and plow caress petite
that swan of angle perpetuity so long
mind time forlorn
that I did it for the ragged patriarchy
and the dead oak men, the
counter sublime of the
fathers with phillips' and wrenches
I wrest these feathers

these girls with bare or hair
these God so tiny fingernails
my sodden chest and appetite
jam band so psychological from if words
I crazy walk must be
I language or steal but pattern
or sidewalk I step Albert
but these same five notes forever
but not count bends like cherries
make stupidly some effort or cool
that cannot be
punishing driven out puella lips
these language television facts
those time I bend there cannot
my feet seem tingle
stool turn blaze carpet jungle
small very a perhaps system analogy
apart sewn walls on
painting K-Mart dissolution
they deserve argyle high school
assholes coffee LSD permissible thirty-eight
long and long so time
just crush she wanted to
me if a there toe connect differentiation
these birds on a wire is mine
but it is in totality my own wire
of dope connect father crying mere dissent
perfection a and pudenda puella
bookbag painted hands now
if I remember correctly Albert
and I with 40s talking
about girls that
is I happen to recollect with
outside time semper
I can still grow ceiling systems
courage defecation crying dignity

she
doesn't
like me she
doesn't
    like
    me
she doesn't like me
and the numb stultus feeling insipid
that you will not devour invoke
or fucking throat nor cry
of words of grey a whole lot of fun
cloud bartenders garbage numbingness
whelming terroreyes telepuella
quintus the dog futuere singsong
error don't I want to fight
mathterpiece breakdown following
I was in the hospital Cuchulain
with a dark Irish
nurse when my hair could reach my blonde
mouth in the many cobblestone
Dogtown Derrida walking
stinking tennis-shoe morning
college girls dumbed on learn
my far-fetcher knife mental
her into I star belief though permissible
fucked situation upon they a don't
retreat but
modern hack weaklings old into
I inhealth against portend
Argus Dogtown flight behold in I situation
all right, things must curtail
it is hell but it is a beautiful hell
all these birds you'll never
know they are not you
I pull at my hammer and pace Delmar

I smile at the Red Sea
I cry Vinegar I smell Lilacs
I perform for you in the windows
your regret fills my balloon I terrorize
that I submit I am your dear
as you walk across the sky with someone else
I wanna go back to being a longshoreman
and ten-thousand Marys on
the docks and I've got my rosary
because big Christ has drunk
me I use my hands on 8th Street
three Puerto Rican dudes push me down the
stairs and break my teeth
so I retreat to Sunnyside and Dogtown
into the closure of the widening
unstopped miracle for destruction
painful Joseph grabbed his mind
bogged down I wove sex
to no particularity kids freezing in
winter bed breath
no baby I'm gonna make
it out all right so I can be straight
with you scene to lifting
so much heavy shit and
yachtsman sitting with a Whiskey Sour
but I have know the nicest men in the world
and I am going to tell you about them
they do not fuck women over anymore
they pick silver gems up off the street
they close each door softly
they do not scream at girls
coming back from McGuirk's who has
the car keys or who paid for how many drinks
they are completely unable to
be assholes for they have
burned in hell and judgment between

wide eyes and when each one
sees a pale girl in a red sweater
at a party in which he
does not fit he looks up afterward and
is forever grateful I know
these guys who would give you a quarter
they are truly mentally ill
not this garbage but have lost everything
Samaritans beyond belief but fat
and original and walked miles in sleet
for fuck's sake pain that has
no word not the bearded coke-head cook
that fucks the line girl in shitty
apartment he chooses aside in West County
indie rock scumbag poseur loser
and with these thoughts
out of the rain and the Mad
at first my feet on another chair
laid back and listening to his call
skoya dibrenka apoeta loserna
asitta how poena tufucka losern
victa hofagga poema
heinherena muta cheappa
mattanya moochskya loserna
buttafuka inskinkska
yanodika lavern tadruska
moocha bustardo poena tadrunka
moocha bustardo poena
pernich persuda hopena
tallentlesta nostudya nopono
cryvitch babooshka
fagota pussino fakyr poetan
lacka penisma tinna pinkish
ton a ton non vernata
butta femaly femalo sturto
tha thy verbosh fucky tunotyo

thy lallentalentno poemy
they mocked and knees weaker I know what they
say and can hear it again
  she doesn't like me
  she
  doesn't
    like
  me she doesn't like me
I found myself looking for mistletoe all night
among the reigns and the crashing
lips my victory
does not have to be gender specific 'cus
I'm a uh soulman of the diffident variety
who turns it on a breathes when
a girl comes along who's already taken
like the Christmas thing in the West End
at first nervous and lonely at the
keg all wired and ready
I'm drinking actual coffee I
brought Ding-Dongs for a spell my
nerves were empty I saw Saint Mary
something about a poor abused-looking
dude so that I am unable to
submit plus I'm not really cute
I'm more like Sartre on a bad hair day
so I told her right away that I like
salad one more sentence I can't account
for I stepped on toes all night triumph
there might have been mistletoe
but I missed it with Barrett and
the high high talk with Holly red lips
I shall in the end my cursing heart
my problem is that I can't shut up
because I opened my garbage and
the words came out of my
head like the newsflashes of 3am

bright as Warhol's hair you'll never
get she said if you
don't know now you'll never know
and I dipped my fingers into
the holy water where five
fierce sisters sat and exclaimed
I was so good and on where there
was no chance of sex shut up
with the flowing hair all around
my barstool when I wanted nothing
but panic at no sex later this
wasted time I forlorn my latent
God, my latent redemption then
return to my homosexual
heart attack under cheap gin and tonic
I with the girl in fur and her
dog that I gave it all up to
try and be authentic you must be
really stupid singing on street corners
and stuff because there was this
old princess who never said shit but
walked around with
motherfucker on her mind all the time,
but with me it's more the
lilting fading sounds of the girls'
ears, expansions diffusions and imbecility—destructions
are all we can compose—
and all the hugging makes
me sort of want to deride columns
caustic and threats forlorn loud
little breasts on my shoulder as if
I were some king of eunuchs
foot-tap mathematics with
lipstick all over my ear, I list
birds my colors and names so also
how they talk so soft to me from

the tree outside the home before the
trip to the movie I confused about
getting laced, looking into the mirror
despair because time is nothing, not
even a puddle, where the riddles refute
the merciless chariot of Mary and young
Tim and me walk back to the car
Jethro Tull Dissociative Disorder
in-and-out nonsense permit me
where it breaks down to fire and name change
expulsive breath and front door kisses
but remember cyclical sodas behind
grey brain tough die on cold teeth concrete

   and she just doesn't like
   one bit when
   she says the bolshevik
   beyond me is
   hot scraggily beard
   two bucks in his pocket
   weighs 100 pounds

I know that creepy is when an
unattractive man acts with confidence
so I put roses and my head down
giraffe big meat deprecations and
abortions down the street but
old women coughing and farting down
in the smoking section is not creepy
or ambulances every five minutes
the loser tapping his feet in music group
with thick long hair non-compliant
subsides completely without language
or if sororities are smarter or dumber
la langue Lacan Derrida dumbfounded
strategies in meaning I meant to say

Phoebe's too young but 'too old'
suddenly slipped out but all along
Delmar I'm thought as a freak ever since
an old lady picking up cigarette butts
is not creepy it is not creepy for a
model to snort coke off a
backseat mirror in the back door cafe
that will be in business for ten minutes
or a cop to step in gum and cross his cousin
it is not creepy to always find a sword
or to die in sex or to trade sex for gin
or to see something new walk
in with a tattered cape surpass intelligence
or to jump out of your
car and chase Lesbia down Grand she
runs into the decrepit dorm and doses
with the guy who sucked Casper off
and threw up on a Teddy Bear likeness
of—wait— I'm really a happy person—if
it is creepy to blow cigar smoke
into someone's face at Powell Hall because
your Lexus runs on blood or see a
false mirror then blood draw with no
bandage after badinage at the nurses' desk
the delusions inside too many other cigarettes
creepy to tap again at that gal we
all know each other is hot but honey if
your residency is in Columbia Missouri
I mean come on I mean come on the
empty bed in the women's hall wake to two-tongue
so to the tin pan alley leanings
of McCartney, the orphean lute,
the Beethoven of Penny Lane,
like when I was drunk on Dale
knowing that when I died desultory
there would be behind these many scribblings,

never to shake hands with Nemerov,
never to stand before to the mic and light,
so to the McCartney of Mozart,
so to the Cyndi Lauper of heaven
and the lament of before this dance is through,
or I've got my mind set on you mathematics,
only because the song did surely end,
and my gloriously Northern Morrissey Wordsworth,
onward the Mozart almost masochistic
in Plato frames from divinity I
Cure pierced my brain and mettle
forgiveness all about the spectre in my arms
my Jakob Dylan structure in my bed
as I floated and sprung I knew Lisa Loeb
I knew Jewell I knew Sarah Cloud
past all belief on hiway 70 CD shattered
so to my Lennon and your Lennon
the grape plucked and thank you girl
Hank Williams liver-spotted in my mind
the Bach and Beethoven of Brown Eyed Girl
the Mahler-on-ecstasy of Brueckner
red carpet concertos Barber
I sang as I could dusty and forlorn
you're the one for me fatty
I'm miserable now Misery Sleepwalker
do you think—yes I do—a million—I
watch the clock as they play
my Madonna John Lee Hooker
my bed was dirty and my beers were empty
five in the morning some guy had
said something up the street I remember
eating pizza in the snow for five
weeks I hung out with this red-headed
gal—she was my Stravinsky—I can't
remember her name—so I went to her
steakhouse I ordered on accident I

crushed myself against the mirror no one
believes me now but Pete Seegar was on
the system I was growing in a maligned
way the two-hearted composition that
took on its own cancer and I stepped out of there
and flagged a rouge taxi and I saw
this snow against a wall looked so warm
and I lay down I was 24 I had three years to live
but would I ever meet that producer who got
everyone high and then insulted them—
because ever since I destroyed my brain
things have become not so clear or
lasting but more confirmed and gentle
so that when I see one shoe
in the street I don't necessarily
have to know absolutely where the
other one is or when my dictionary
just becomes fun and I don't say
I must use 'gymnastic' or 'cupidity'
but love me alone my island
I was walking in below zero just
a t-shirt and drunk to the ATM
on Fifth and there was a shriveled
woman pregnant on a trashbag
lying there naked I repose and recuse
she—I tell you I have no meaning—all
out of proportion time mistake
these cheddar burgers I can't forget
when the smell of my brothers ZBT
French hooker who taught me plain
speech and clarified Missouri
for me am I sorry about immense
fortunes I've had from free bongs
and the girls I will tentatively name
pernod passion one anecdote is a good
and as another and obviously yo you I do

not pick economics I pick reference and
somewhat love starry-eyed
the tunnels I've been trapped in and not
to forget about Lesbia: I went back
to retrieve my broken flowers and
all around was the sense of wetness
or the beautiful gal cleaning our tub
told me not to come up but I came up a
year later she wanted and described me
so I threw a snowball at her when the
drive was cascaded and became more complicated
life is not really
life when you think about it we do
as the visions stronger white furniture
in my dorm with seven Colins smoking
me out uttered before near expulsion a
Picasso ripoff on the wall I was
crying at the cops and firemen I'd never be
and suddenly I feel that
painting I understand stairs you can trip on
should we dance to this off time now
really I think I can dance anywhere
to anything it all makes mute sense
I can believe I wore those cowboy boots
and had some hooker on speed dial

    and so she doesn't and
    if she
    doesn't well she don't
    I forget
    what do I remember
    no one (everyone)
    likes me I like me my
    shoes and hair if I
    don't
    look in the mirror and

at any photograph my
Brad Pitt sophia mind

Platonic Mary took me to the park
where bread played for pigeons
when I explained I was (this ain't
a journal) astounded
she trained a poor pale boy to make salad
I like salad I said but I thought you
discourse/construct discourse/construct
construct/discourse construct/discourse
we are so inveterate that
we could certainly be related
proud Platonic Mary of Memory
not you but when we were kids
I could see someone's mole I
never even knowed her but perfect
sentences from
the 60's when you were a pretty
nun and I snuck beer into the convent
and teased your feet and climbed your tree
we almost did it and figure before
I confessed I fucked five girls
but I was housed and homeless
reading the Kabbalah
in some girls' Chinese room
so many wasted I is another
how many cops I walked up Broadway love
insane ZBT posse still love me
I never have shouted again
like I did then the sap and strive
more visceral walking along on
the Boulevard of Broken Discourse
taking two and two apart
that's where we lie Platonic Leaves
I would give five hands for your finger

but excuse me please if
this is a bunch of castration
or introjection or projection I don't know if
I go to MPC again no take me to Barnes
but please call
Harold Bloom and prenatal guilt
because the dignity of work
can kiss the discourse of my ass when
the only real consolation is
that everyone else is fucking stupid
even so if I woke up hog-tied
and no idea what city I was in
everything I love destroyed
every time I touch the door I shock
like a little electric prick
which I also pun but no sweetie
OMD castration anxiety gas station
cigarette down to the rose petals
that the albatross shit—Father can it be—yes
it is all true threatened
by a short thin clerk fifteen
plus beef jerky tense I'm a girl the
mocking horror can't hold back art student
light from the beer sign suddenly a symptom
so that further explanation is impossible
I is a great big ghost that
took the steps out of the stairs
and railed against the railing
took the dancer out of the dance
took the quiddity out of the quizzical nada
the girls I loved
are in penthouses now on Lake Shore Drive
sure it's easy if the mind's
but not this I am thought
intelligence of the bleating bar
scraggily-bearded bullshit and botox waitress

liquor store communion falsify
(if there ain't a plot there ain't snot)
(dibs on the blonde) and
every man must till the earth
where shadow plaints are held at zero worth
from blistered hands and ruddy faces
my crabboat pencil and hardened page
you know I love dropping names so
I'll say now I must be a born-again virgin
if this Real is to pass nigh near
someone who wants to force me to speak French
I swear insane brainstorming freakout
Platonic Mary with Jewish hair and allegory
Tithonus vibe from me un-hitting upon
here I am an athlete with new girls
leaning towards the gate of my myth
impossible frameworks I've loosened again
on the funeral of
her sex and the ashes of her breast
I'm so sexual it almost creates a lack
a vacuum between the legs of eternity
(and I've got a million fucking dollars)
that places my code of ethics as
a ruler that curves towards
by bellybutton bursting with a lack
the queen of realism smelling and swearing
the nipples changing hands by the minute

   I told you dude she don't
   like you why are you doing
   this she ain't interested in you
   this is borderline creepy you're
   no fucking Joyce I don't see it
   be careful with the Kabbalah

cross legged on a motel room bed confession

candy bars and Diet Dr Pepper
air conditioning at last student loans
I didn't really want to get to know her
pony dreams and the fake no-talent ass-clown
Morrissey wannabe who went
down on some dude and threw up
and I wake to a pattern that's set in stone
and I beg of His mercy as the bars come down
the diffident space of the dark night done
her vapid symptomology wedding that
everything's a metaphor for everything else
walk a mile with this nice watch on asshole
as I ventured down the yellow highway
and my wall clock was back under the safe
I stepped in mud and saw
a virgin in lace with white
wrists and perfect teeth morph
into some type of hairy wolf and
I tried in vain to give it up while
she came and struggled against me
so I threw my coat over the puddle
and the coat turned into a
curtain that opened to show a bare
microphone facing an empty concert house
I writhed in agony upon the stage
I could not reach the summit elevator
I was trapped in on the 8th floor
falling faster and faster into
the highest boom relaxation technique
softly so louder and louder into my ear peace
unutterable drum groups and stretching seminars
high talking or language secrets
or shifting innuendo or doubletalking
or deuterohermeneuticality or razor grains
or bleeding feet or busting side or purple face

Holy shit God sat next to
me in the form of some guy living in
his car cashing his check in the bar
dollar drafts had I drank again an exploration
of the drive he says considers
a half-assed dick and limp ideas of
reference more and more the wonders are
coming across appears and dead pedestrians
your desperate longing you
will never get laid again
God the pressure's off and she
always liked you she always
wanted you she gave you hint after
hint because of your ascet shame
the blown-up sun and spoken glass
you are so afraid of nothing
put your hands in your pants
as the signs and wonders
increase and revolve all you
think about her and in time
go back to forms go back to
time recess and torn apart
say your last crippled words
and woo her in reverse.

www.ingramcontent.com/pod-product-compliance
Lightning Source LLC
Chambersburg PA
CBHW011421070526
44584CB00026BA/3787